The Voyage of
Saint Brendan
In a Modern English Version
by Simon Webb

Published by the Langley Press, 2015

© 2015 Simon Webb. The right of Simon Webb to be identified as the Author of the Work has been asserted by him in accordance with the Copyright, Designs and Patents Act 1988. All rights reserved.

The cover shows a detail of an illumination in: Peraldus: *Theological miscellany, including the Summa de vitiis,* England, second or third quarter of the thirteenth century, after c. 1236. British Library Harley MS 3244

Also from the Langley Press:

The Voyage of Saint Brendan by William Caxton
The Legend of St Cuthbert
In Search of the Northern Saints
In Search of Bede
In Search of St Alban
Gilbert's Tale: The Life and Death of Thomas Becket
Nicholas Breakspear: The Pope From England
Bede's Life of St Cuthbert

For free downloads, and for more books from the Langley Press, please visit our website at:

http://tinyurl.com/lpdirect

Contents

Introduction	5
I. Brendan Before his Voyage	11
II. The Voyage of Saint Brendan	19
III. Brendan After His Voyage	64
Further Reading	76

Introduction

When the conditions are just right, it is sometimes possible to see near the horizon things that just can't be there. These mirages, sometimes known as *Fata Morgana*, remind us how we rely on light to perceive things with our eyes, and also demonstrate that light itself can deceive us.

Before these phenomena were understood scientifically, mariners, islanders and travellers through deserts and in the polar regions were sometimes fooled into thinking that there were castles, rivers, lakes, cities, mountains, and islands, complete with buildings, vegetation, people and livestock, shimmering on the horizon.

A phantom island was often seen by inhabitants of the Canary Islands, who, in the words of Washington Irving, 'fancied they beheld a mountainous island, of about ninety leagues in length, lying far to the westward. It was only seen at intervals, though in perfectly clear and serene weather. To some it seemed one hundred leagues distant, to others forty, to others only fifteen or eighteen'.

The reason why the phantom island of the Canary Islanders is relevant to this book is that 'the name of St Brendan was from time immemorial given to this imaginary island, for when the rumour circulated of such a place . . . the legends of St Brendan were revived, and applied to this unapproachable land'.

The fact that the name of a saint from the west of Ireland, nearly two thousand miles to the north, should have been applied to a phenomenon observed from a group of islands off the coast of Africa attests not only to the international character of the Roman Catholic Church in general, but to the popularity of St Brendan in particular.

Far to the north, the Irish of the Atlantic coast had their own illusory island, but they called theirs Hy-Brasil. It is likely that some features of some of the islands seen and visited by St Brendan owe something to ideas about this particular mirage. An island supported on pillars mentioned in the Latin Life of Brendan springs to mind. The tricks that can be played by these mirages include the one of turning objects upside-down. Since, as we have seen in the case of St Brendan's Isle, it is hard to estimate distances of objects seen in a mirage, it is likely that some observers on the coast of Ireland mistook the images of ships with masts, inverted, for islands on stilts.

If the fleeting visions of the *Fata Morgana* and the stories they generated are one source for the strange places described in tales of St Brendan, sea-stories featuring heroes other than monks must also have contributed to the fantastical contents of the saint's voyage.

In the Irish tradition, sea-stories are known as *immrama*, and the *immram* of Máel Dúin in particular shares many features with Brendan's voyage. This suggests that their respective authors influenced each other, or perhaps that the tales of Máel Dúin and Brendan share a common ancestor.

Brendan sets out from Ireland in search of the Land of the Promise of the Saints, but Máel Dúin is looking for the man who killed his father. Like Brendan, Máel Dúin constructs a sort of giant coracle covered with animal skins for his journey.

Máel Dúin is about to set off with a certain number of companions, when three extra men use emotional blackmail to force their way onto his boat, as also happens to Brendan. Like Brendan, Máel Dúin is forced to visit many islands and witness many strange sights before he can get to his ultimate destination; and many of the phenomena Máel Dúin witnesses are reminiscent of those seen by Brendan and his monks.

Máel Dúin encounters a number of hermits whose only clothing is their own hair, and he also sees animals and people that are much larger than usual. Like Brendan, Máel Dúin passes close to an island colonised by blacksmiths, and both explorers are pelted with lumps of hot material thrown by giant smiths.

The fact that the crews of both Brendan and Máel Dúin's eat or drink things that send them into comas suggests that both of these tales may have been influenced by the ninth book of Homer's *Odyssey*, where Odysseus's crew eat the narcotic lotos plant and decline into an apathetic daze.

It might seem unlikely that ancient Greek literature could have influenced old Irish tales, but the tenth-century Latin *Navigatio Brendani* which is the primary source for Brendan's voyage was almost certainly written by a monk, and such a man, fluent enough in Latin to write a book in that language, could easily have known about the *Odyssey*, and even read it in the original Greek.

As well as the *immrama*, and perhaps older, classical literature, the *Navigatio* may owe some of its content to garbled reports of actual voyages made by Brendan and others.

The Island of the Smiths, where Brendan's boat is pelted with hot slag, may be derived from a real visit to an erupting volcano, or volcanic island. Likewise, the mysterious crystal pillar encountered by Brendan may originally have been an iceberg (Máel Dúin sees a silver pillar).

We now know that there were Viking settlers in Newfoundland, and that the Vikings called this place Vinland because of the grapes, or more likely berries, that grew there. Tales of this distant, fruitful land may have transformed themselves into the tale of the giant grapes, each yielding a pound of juice, gathered by Brendan's monks.

The possibility that Brendan, or other voyagers using the maritime technology he knew, could have travelled as far as the North American continent was explored by Tim Severin in his Brendan voyage of 1976-7. In a boat covered with tanned ox-hides, Severin and his crew managed to reach Peckford Island off Newfoundland, having set off from the west of Ireland.

Although the stories of Brendan's voyage and of his life on dry land must have been compiled from diverse sources, including details of the real life of this sixth-century Irish abbot, it is possible to discern a distinctive character in Brendan, at least in the incidents included in this book.

He is brave, resourceful and determined, and seems to possess the kind of charisma that makes a good leader. He is attractive enough as a personality to inspire people to follow him, to welcome him when he arrives, even unexpectedly, and to long for his presence, when he is absent. This attractiveness becomes a problem for the saint early in the story of his voyage, when he acquires three extra voyagers over and above the number he has carefully chosen.

Alongside his natural gifts as an attractive leader, Brendan has certain supernatural gifts, because, after all, he is a saint. He is able to perform miracles, including raising the dead, and to some extent he is able to prophesy future events. He is also able to see and understand certain things more clearly than his fellow-travellers, who by comparison can sometimes seem a little foolish. He knows perfectly well that the island that proves to be a giant fish is what it is, and remains on his boat while his monks set about making a fire on Jasconius's back.

As well as the qualities that make him appear naturally and supernaturally powerful, Brendan has certain weaknesses that surprise the reader, but make his character seem more real and sympathetic. He is easily humbled and moved to tears, though we must remember that in those days before ideas about the 'stiff upper lip', men would express their emotions more openly.

Since he always has one eye on heaven, Brendan can also be blunt and insensitive in his dealings with those who are more worldly. He doesn't hesitate to tell the 'additional' monks who join him at the start of his voyage that two of them will come to a bad end, and his impatience with the brother of a monk who is supposed to be watching his boat causes the man's death. When he realises what he has done, Brendan is compelled to set out on another voyage, not of exploration, but to find forgiveness.

It is made clear in some of the tales of Brendan printed in this book that Brendan was not supposed to be the best, or ideal, monk or saint. He is humbled by the perfection some of the religious people he encounters have achieved; and he learns that to beg the help of God in the name of St Brendan is not always as effectual as an appeal to the more perfect St Brigid.

Brendan's restlessness, his impatience and his occasional hot temper may go some way to explain why, when he eventually reaches the Land of the Promise of the Saints, he isn't allowed to stay there very long.

The modern English version of the *Navigatio Brendani* that makes up the bulk of this book sticks closely to the version published by Denis O'Donoghue in his *Brendaniana* (Browne & Nolan, 1893).

To modernise the text, I have broken up many of O'Donoghue's long sentences, and replaced many of his long and/or antiquated words with shorter, more modern equivalents. I have also replaced the canonical times used by the original author, such as 'prime', with modern times such as 'nine o'clock'. In a very few places, I have inserted explanations in square brackets. The sections derived from the Irish and Latin Lives of St Brendan are compilations of some of the more interesting sections of these biographies, again from *Brendaniana*.

The fact that the original *Navigatio* would have been re-copied by hand, and ultimately derives from a number of sources, explains some of the repetitions that I have silently excluded. The process of its composition and transmission probably explains some of the obvious mistakes in the text, which I have allowed to stand. One of these occurs in the account of the island where a dog leads Brendan and his monks to a great hall where they enjoy a sumptuous feast. In the version O'Donoghue uses, it is clear that a section is missing, which must have described how the feast appeared, or was brought to, the voyagers.

SW, Durham, December 2014

I. Brendan Before His Voyage

(From the Irish Life of St Brendan in the Book of Lismore)

Brendan was born in the days of Ænguis, son of Nathfraech, the king of Munster in Ireland. He was from a place called Kerry-Luachra in the district of Alltraighe-Cuile. His father, Finnlugh, was a noble man, honest and religious. He and his wife owed allegiance to a bishop called Erc.

Before he was born, Brendan's mother had a vision. She saw her bosom full of pure gold, and her breasts glistening white as snow. When she told her vision to Bishop Erc, he said, 'You are going to give birth to a child of power, who will be full of the grace of the Holy Spirit.'

A rich man called Airde, son of Fidach, lived at some distance from the house of Finnlugh, and an Irish prophet called Becc MacDé lived with him in his mansion.

Airde asked Becc, 'What unknown event is going to happen here soon?'

Becc answered, 'Tonight your true and worthy king will be born, between you and the sea. Many kings and princes will honour him, and he will carry those kings and princes with him to heaven.'

On the night of Brendan's birth, thirty cows belonging to Airde MacFidaigh gave birth to thirty heifer calves.

Next day Airde got up early, and went to look for the house where the child was born. He found the baby at the house of Finnlugh: he knelt before the child, and gave him the thirty cows with their thirty calves. This was the first gift made to Brendan. Then this great land-holder took the child in his arms, and said, 'Let this child be my foster-son forever.'

Now on the night that Brendan was born, Bishop Erc saw that the whole of Alltraighe-Cuile was bathed in an extraordinary blaze of light, a thing that he had never seen before. He also saw various ministering angels in snow-white robes all around the district.

In the morning he rose early, and went to the house of Finnlugh. Taking the child in his arms, he said, 'Oh, man of God, accept me as your faithful follower. Many will rejoice at your birth, just as my heart and soul now greatly rejoice.' Then he lay face-down in front of Brendan, and sobbed for joy. Soon he baptised him: the name Mobbi was given to him at first, as this was the name his parents had chosen.

Later a white mist came down, and spread over everything. Because of this, he was re-named 'Broenfinn', meaning 'White Mist'.

A miracle happened during his baptism: three purple sheep leaped out of the font. These were the fee for Brendan's baptism.

His family then took him with them, so that he could drink his mother's milk for a year. Then Bishop Erc took him to his foster-mother St Ita, where he remained for five years. Ita was a nun, and she loved him very much. She saw angels all round him, helping him; and she could tell that the Holy Spirit was always with him.

Whenever Brendan saw Ita, he would be happy and cry out to her. One day Ita asked him, 'What is making you so joyful, my holy child?'

'You,' he said. 'I see you talking to me all the time, like all the other virgins who are always nursing me.' The other virgins that he saw were angels disguised as virgins.

Later Brendan read the psalms with Bishop Erc for five years, and Ita missed him very much.

Now Bishop Erc couldn't afford to keep a cow that gave milk, because he lived only on what his faithful flock could afford to give him. One day, he wanted milk for his foster-child, and he said, 'God is able to provide it, my son.' Sure enough, after this a wild cow came every day with its calf from Slieve-luachra, to be milked for Brendan.

In those days Brendan's sister Brig lived with him. Brendan loved her very much, and he could see angels all round her, helping her. He could also see that the face of his foster-father, the bishop, shone like the summer sun.

When Brendan was ten years of age, Bishop Erc took him on a missionary journey, to preach the Word of God.

While the clergy were preaching, Brendan was left alone in a cart, where he sat reading the psalms. Then a young flaxen-haired girl came up and admired his face, which was beautiful and bright. Although the girl was gentle and modest, and came from a princely family, she jumped into the cart, hoping to play some childish game with Brendan.

But Brendan said, 'Go home: you should never have been left here.' Then he grabbed the reins of the cart and gave the girl a severe flogging with them, until she was crying and bawling.

She ran back to the place where her parents, the king and queen, were staying. When Bishop Erc returned, he told Brendan that he shouldn't have beaten the little girl, and in no uncertain terms.

'I will do penance for it,' said the saint; 'and you should tell me what penance I should do.'

'Very well,' said Erc. 'Go into that cave there, and stay there alone until I come back tomorrow.'

So Brendan went and sat in the cave, and began to sing his psalms and his hymns of praise to the Lord. Bishop Erc hid beside the cave, listening to Brendan, without his knowing it.

The sound of Brendan's voice, chanting the psalms, was heard for the distance of a thousand paces on every side. (The voice of Saint Columba was heard for the same distance when he was chanting his psalms and hymns.)

While Brendan was in the cave, people saw troops of angels flying up to heaven and down to earth, all around the cave, until morning. After that night, no one could look at Brendan's face for very long, because it shined so brightly. Only Finan Cam could stare at it, because he himself was full of the grace of the Holy Spirit.

One day, Brendan and Bishop Erc were on a journey when a young man fell in with them along the way. As they went along, some enemies of the young man blocked their path. They were seven warriors, and the young man trembled with fear and said, 'These men will murder me.'

'Keep walking,' said Brendan, 'and when you get to it, lie down in the shadow of that stone.' The young man did as Brendan told him, and Brendan raised his hands to God, and prayed that the stone, which was in the shape of a pillar, would start to look like the young man. The seven warriors came to the pillar-stone, stabbed it, then cut off the top of it. Then they carried the top of the stone away, thinking that it was the head of the young man. What's left of the pillar-stone is still there, and you can see it yourself if you're clever enough to find it. This is the story of how Brendan made a man out of a stone, and a stone out of a man.

Bishop Erc told the young man to do penance, and to give thanks, 'For the head of the stone that you have, and also give thanks that your enemies went away without hurting you.' Later, both Brendan and the young man did penance.

After Brendan had learned the Old Testament and the New, he wanted to write down and learn the Rules of all of the saints of Ireland. Bishop Erc gave him permission to do this, because he knew that God had put the idea in Brendan's head. The bishop said to him, 'Come back to me when you have learned those Rules, so that I can make you a priest.'

Brendan went and asked his foster-mother Ita about this, and she said the same to him; 'Yes, learn the Rules of the Saints of Ireland, but do not learn them from women or virgins, because that could look suspicious. But go, and on your way you will meet a charming, noble soldier.'

After Brendan had been travelling for a short time, he met just such a man, who was called Colman Mac Lenin. Brendan said to him, 'Do penance, because God is calling you! He wants you to be a dutiful son to him.' That was when Colman became a Christian, and he eventually built a church on the spot where he had met Brendan.

Later, Brendan went to Connaught, because he wanted

to meet a famous holy man called Iarlath, son of Lug. Iarlath taught Brendan all the Rules of the saints of Ireland.

Once, Brendan said to Iarlath, 'You will not be buried here, so on the Day of Judgement your body will not rise from here.'

'My holy son,' said Iarlath, 'you mustn't make a secret out of the divine graces of the Holy Spirit that are obviously in you, or the countless powers of the Lord Almighty that lie secretly in your spotless soul. You came here to learn from me, but now *you* will be *my* master. Please, tell me where I will be buried and resurrected.'

Brendan replied, 'Order a new carriage to be made for you, worthy of a bishop, then set off in it on your travels. At the place where the two shafts of the carriage break, that will be the place of your resurrection, and the resurrection of many other people along with you.'

Soon, the bishop set off in his new carriage, and after he had travelled for a short time, both of the shafts broke. The place where this happened was called Tuaim-daghualann.

When Brendan left Iarlath, he set off for the plain of Ai. An angel met him on the road, who said, 'Write down what I am about to tell you: I am going to tell you the Rules of the religious life.'

So Brendan wrote down all the angel's holy Rules, and the list Brendan made still exists.

When Brendan was travelling across the plain of Ai, he saw the body of a dead man on a bier. All his friends were following the bier and mourning for the young man.

'Put your trust in the Lord,' said Brendan, 'and the dead man will be restored to life.'

After Brendan had prayed to God, the young man came back to life, and his family joyfully took him home.

After this, all the people began to stare at Brendan whenever they saw him, and they took him to meet the king of the plain. The king offered him land in whatever part of the plain he wanted, but Brendan refused the offer, because he didn't want to stay there.

When Brendan had written down the Rules the angel dictated to him, and the Rules of all the saints of Ireland, together with their customs and ways of praying, he went back to Bishop Erc, and was made a priest. It was then that he read in the Gospel, 'Everyone who has left father, or mother, or sister, or lands, shall receive a hundred-fold in this present time, and shall possess life everlasting.'

After that, the love of the Lord grew and grew in Brendan's heart, and he longed to leave his own country, and his family. One day, he begged the Lord to give him some place; secret, retired, secure, delightful, away from other people.

That night, he heard the voice of an angel from heaven, saying to him, 'Arise, Brendan; God will grant you what you prayed for – he will give you the Land of Promise.'

So Brendan got up, and felt happy because of what the angel had said. He went on his own to Brandon Hill and looked out over the vast and gloomy ocean which lay around him on every side. In that place, he had a vision of a beautiful noble island, where angels would help him.

He stayed at Brandon Hill for three days, and fell asleep. Then the angel of the Lord came to talk to him, and said, 'From now on I will stay with you for ever and ever, and I will teach you how to find the beautiful island that you saw in your vision.'

At this, Brendan sobbed for joy, and thanked God with all his heart.

II. The Voyage of Saint Brendan (from the *Navigatio Brendani*)

Saint Brendan, son of Finnlug Ua Alta, was born in the marshy district of Munster. He became famous because of his great abstinence and his many other virtues, and he was an abbot; father to nearly three thousand monks.

While he was fighting his spiritual war, at a place called Ardfert-Brendan, he was visited one evening by a priest called Barinthus, who was a relative of King Niall.

When Brendan asked Barinthus questions, his visitor couldn't talk properly: all he could do was weep, and stretch himself out on the ground, and pray.

Brendan pulled him up, hugged him, and said, 'Father, why are you so upset? Surely you have visited us to bring us comfort! You're upsetting the other monks! In God's name, tell us what you know, and refresh our souls with stories of your adventures at sea!'

And so Barinthus told them about a certain island.

'My dear son, Mernoc, who was the almoner at our monastery, left us to become a hermit. He found an island near the Stone Mountain: it was an island full of delights. After a while, I learned that he was the leader of many monks who lived there, and that he had done many miracles by the power of God. So I went to visit him, and when I was about three days' sailing away, he sailed out and met me in the middle of the sea, with some of his brothers: God had told him that we were coming.

'As we drew near the island, the monks all came out of their cells, like a swarm of bees. They lived in separate cells, but they all got along with each other, because they all had faith, hope, and love. They ate together in one refectory, and prayed and conducted services in one church.

'The monks there only ate fruit and nuts, roots and other vegetables. After compline, they passed the night in their separate cells until the cock-crow, or when the bell tolled for prayer. When my dear son and I had crossed the island on foot, he led me to the western shore, where there was a small boat. There he said, "Father, enter this boat, and we will sail on to the west, towards the island called the Land of the Promise of the Saints, which God will give to the next generation."

'When we were under sail, dense clouds surrounded us, so that we could hardly see the prow or the stern of the boat. After an hour or so, a bright light shone all around us, and we saw land. The island was big and grassy, and there were all sorts of fruits growing there.

'When the boat touched the shore, we got out, and then we explored the island for fifteen days; but there was always more to see. All the plants there had flowers on them, all the trees had fruit, and every stone was a precious gem.

'On the fifteenth day we discovered a river flowing from west to east. We didn't know how to cross the river, so we waited for advice from God. While we were waiting, a man suddenly appeared in front of us. He was shining with a bright light, and he called us by our names, and said, "Welcome, worthy brothers, for the Lord has revealed to you the land He will give to His saints. This river divides the land in two, and you are not permitted to cross it. You must go back where you came from."

'We asked the man his name, and where he came from, but he just said, "Why do you ask these questions? You should ask me about this island instead. It has stayed just as it is now from the beginning of the world. Have you been hungry or thirsty since you came here? Have you felt tired, or seen the sun go down? Of course not! It is always daytime here, and never night. The endless light comes from the Lord Jesus Christ, and if people could only have avoided sin, they would have lived here forever."

'When we heard this, we were all moved to tears. We rested awhile, then we set out for the shore, escorted by the man who had spoken to us.

'We got into our boat, and as we did so the man who had spoken to us disappeared. We sailed through the thick mist we had encountered before, and then reached the Island of Delights. The monks there were very happy to see that we had returned safely, as they had been very sad to see us go. They asked, "Why, our fathers, did you leave us, your little flock, to stray about without a shepherd in the wilderness?"

'When I heard this I tried to console them, and said, "Brothers, do not be troubled: your lives here are lived near the gates of paradise. Not far from here lies the island of the Land of the Promise of the Saints, where it is always day, and never night. The angels of God watch over that place, and your abbot, Mernoc, lives there. Can't you tell from the lovely smell of our clothes that we have just come back from the paradise of God?"

'They replied, "Yes, father, we know where you've been, because our abbot often had that smell about him.

Sometimes the smell would hang around for nearly forty days."

'Then I told them that we had lived there with my dear son for a fortnight, without food or drink; yet we felt neither hungry nor thirsty.

'After forty days, we left that island with the blessing of the abbot and the monks, so that I could return again to my little cell. I will go there tomorrow.'

When they had heard all this from Barinthus, their visitor, Brendan and his monks threw themselves on the ground, giving glory to God in these words, 'Righteous You are, O Lord, in all Your ways, and holy in all Your works, who has revealed to Your children so many great wonders; and blessed be You for Your gifts, who has this day refreshed us all with this spiritual feast.'

When everything was quiet again, Brendan said, 'Let's eat: but first I must wash everyone's feet.'

The next morning St Barinthus received the blessing of all the monks, and set off back to his own cell.

Brendan quickly picked out fourteen monks from his whole community. He took these into an oratory, where he said to them, 'Dearly beloved comrades in arms, I need your advice, and your help. I've decided: if it is God's will, I am going to find this Land of the Promise of the Saints that Father Barinthus told us about. What do you think?'

The monks replied, 'Father abbot, we will do whatever you ask. Didn't we all leave our parents and our heritage to join you? Haven't we put ourselves entirely in your hands? Of course we are ready to go with you, if God wills it, whether you lead us to life or death.'

Brendan, and the monks he had chosen, decided to fast for forty days before they set out. At the end of the forty days, Brendan said a fond farewell to the monks he was leaving behind, and commended them to the special care of the prior of his monastery. This prior also took over from Brendan as abbot, when Brendan died. And so Brendan and his fourteen monks sailed west to the island of St Enda, and remained there for three days and three nights.

Enda blessed his visitors and their journey, and Brendan sailed back to the mainland, to the region where his parents still lived. He didn't visit his parents, but set off for a remote part of the country, and climbed to the top of the mountain that is now called St Brendan's Seat. This mountain is on a piece of land that stretches far out into the ocean. There Brendan put up a tent, near a narrow creek, where a boat could enter.

In this place, Brendan and his companions used their iron tools to put together a light vessel, with wicker sides and ribs. This is a type of boat that is often seen in that area: they covered it with cow-hide, tanned in oak-bark, and painted the joints with tar. They loaded enough provisions for forty days, including butter to dress the hides that covered the boat. They also took with them all the tools that they would need for their journey.

Brendan then ordered all the monks to get on board, in the name of the Father, the Son, and the Holy Spirit.

While Brendan stood on the shore and blessed the little creek, three more monks from his monastery came up. They threw themselves at his feet, and cried out: 'Oh dearest father, for the love of Christ, let us come with you on your voyage. If you don't let us come, we'll starve ourselves to death, because we are determined to stay with you for ever'

When the saint saw how desperate they were, he told them to get on board, but he said, 'I know why you have come here. One of you has made a good decision, and he will be rewarded by God; but the other two will suffer His judgement.'

Then St Brendan got on board, and they set sail for the summer solstice. They had a good wind, which meant that they had little work to do: they just had to keep the sails properly set. But after twelve days the wind fell away and they were becalmed. This meant that they had to row like mad to make any progress, and they were soon exhausted.

At times like this, Brendan would encourage them by crying out, 'Fear not, brothers, for our God will help us! He will be our pilot! Ship the oars and leave the rudder alone: keep the sails set, and may God steer our little vessel where He will.'

They always ate in the evening, and sometimes a wind sprung up at that time; but they didn't know which direction it came from, or where it was taking them.

At the end of forty days, when they had eaten all their food, they spotted a steep, rocky island to the north. They sailed closer, and saw that it had steep cliffs like giant walls, and many streams of water rushing down into the sea; but they couldn't find a place to land their boat.

They were very thirsty as well as hungry, and they tried to catch the water from the streams in anything they thought would hold water. But Brendan warned them, 'Brothers! Don't be so stupid! If God doesn't want us to land here, he won't want us to drink the water. Wait for three days: then Jesus Christ will show us a safe place to land: a place where you can both eat and drink!'

When they had sailed round the island for three days, they saw a small cove at about three o'clock in the afternoon. It had high, steep, rocky sides like walls, but it looked like a good landing-place, and Brendan stood up in the boat and blessed it.

When they were all on the beach, Brendan was telling the brothers to leave everything in the boat, when a dog appeared, walking along a little path. The dog fawned on the saint, as if Brendan were his master.

'The Lord has sent us a good messenger; let's follow him,' said Brendan, and the monks followed the dog until they came to a large mansion. Inside they found a spacious hall, with couches and seats, and water for washing their feet. There were also vessels made of various types of metal hanging round the walls, and bridle-bits, and drinking-horns inlaid with silver.

When they had rested in the hall for a while, Brendan warned them to beware, 'Because Satan might lead you into temptation. I can see him now, trying to tempt one of the three monks who joined us at the last moment. The Devil's trying to get him to steal something. Pray for his soul, brothers – his body is already in Satan's power.'

Brendan ordered the monk who waited on them to serve up the meal God had sent, and soon the table was laid with napkins, and with white loaves, and fish for each brother. When everything was ready, Brendan blessed the food and the assembled monks, saying, 'Let us give praise to the God of heaven, who provides food for all His creatures.'

Then the brothers ate and drank as much as they

pleased, giving thanks to the Lord. When the meal was finished, and Mass had been heard, Brendan said, 'It's time to rest now; here you can see couches prepared for each of you, and you need to rest your limbs. You're all worn out after the tough time we've had at sea.'

When the brothers were all asleep, Brendan saw a demon, disguised as a little dark-skinned boy, up to no good. He had a bridle-bit in his hands and was beckoning to the monk he was trying to tempt. After he had seen this, Brendan rose from his couch, and prayed all night.

When morning came the brothers were keen to say their prayers and get into their boat again. They found the table laid for their breakfast, as it had been for dinner the night before. In this way, God provided for His servants for three days and three nights.

As they made their way to their boat, Brendan warned them not to take anything from the island.

'God forbid that any of us should dishonour our journey by theft,' the monks replied.

Then Brendan said, 'Look at the brother I warned you about last night. He has a silver bridle-bit hidden under his clothes. The devil gave him that, last night.'

When the brother in question heard this, he threw the bridle-bit away and fell at the feet of the saint, crying out, 'Oh father, I am guilty! Forgive me, and pray that I don't lose my soul!'

Then all the brothers cast themselves on the ground, begging the Lord to save his soul. When they got up, Brendan raised up the guilty brother, and they all saw a little dark-skinned boy leap out from under his clothes, howling.

'Man of God, why have you forced me out of my

home?' cried the devil. 'I have lived here for seven years, yet you drive me away, as if I were a stranger! That place was mine!'

'I command you,' Brendan replied, 'in the name of the Lord Jesus Christ, that you hurt nobody else until the Day of Judgement!' Turning to the guilty monk, he told him to get ready to receive the body and blood of Jesus, because his soul would soon depart from his body. He also told him that he would be buried there on the island. He added that the other monk who had joined them at the last minute would he buried in hell.

Sure enough, the monk who had stolen the silver bit was soon dead, and his soul was taken up to heaven by angels of light. His brothers saw this, and then they gave him a Christian burial on the island.

Brendan and the brothers came to the place where their boat was waiting for them, and got in straight away. Before they set off, a young man appeared, carrying a basket full of loaves of bread, and a large bottle of water. The young man said, 'Accept this blessing from me, your servant, because you have a long way to go before you find the comfort you are looking for. This bread and water will last till Pentecost.' After this blessing, they sailed out into the ocean, eating only every second day, while the boat was blown about in different directions.

One day they spotted another island, not far off, and a favourable wind pushed them towards it. When the boat reached a landing-place, Brendan ordered everyone to get out before he did. They walked all round the island, and saw great streams of water flowing from many fountains, full of all kinds of fish. Brendan said 'Let us celebrate the

Mass here, for this day is the festival of the Lord's Supper.' [Maundy Thursday.] They remained on this island until Easter Saturday.

They found many flocks of pure white sheep on the island: in fact there were so many that it was hard to see the ground between them. The saint told the monks to catch one sheep for their Maundy Thursday feast. They caught one and tied a rope around its horns, but it followed them very calmly, like a tame animal.

They started to prepare for the Maundy Thursday service, which was to happen the next day, when a man appeared with a basket of hearth-cakes [baked in the ashes of a fire] and other provisions. These he laid at the feet of the saint, stretching himself out on the ground three times, and saying, with tears, 'Oh, precious pearl of God, how have I deserved this, that I can give you food I have made myself, for you to eat at your holy festival.'

Brendan helped the man up and said, 'My Son, our Lord Jesus Christ has provided a suitable place for us to celebrate His holy resurrection.'

Later, the saint continued to prepare for the next day's festival. When the supply of provisions had been loaded onto Brendan's ship, the man who had brought them said to him, 'Your boat can carry no more now, but after eight days I will send you enough food and drink to last until Pentecost.'

Then Brendan asked him, 'How can you know for certain where we will be after eight days?' and the man replied, 'You will spend tonight on the island that you can see over there: in fact you will stay there until noon tomorrow. Then you will sail on to another island a little to the west, called the Paradise of Birds; and you will stay there until eight days after Pentecost.'

Brendan also asked him why the sheep were so large on that island, even larger than oxen. He told him that they were larger because they were never milked, and did not go hungry in winter-time, because there was always plenty of grass for them to eat.

Then the monks got back into their ship, and after giving and receiving fond farewells, they continued their voyage.

When they drew near to the nearest island, the boat stopped before they could reach a landing-place, and the saint ordered the brothers to get out into the sea, and make the ship fast, stem and stern, until they came to some harbour.

There was no grass on the island, very little wood, and no sand on the shore. While the brothers spent the night in prayer, the saint remained on the ship, because he knew what type of island this was. He didn't want to tell the other monks, in case they became afraid.

When morning dawned, he ordered the priests to celebrate Mass, and after they had done so, and he himself had said Mass in the boat, the monks took out some uncooked meat and fish they had brought from the other island, and put a cauldron on a fire to cook them.

After they had added more fuel to the fire, and the cauldron began to boil, the island moved about like a wave; so they all rushed towards the boat, and begged Brendan to protect them. Brendan took each one by the hand and pulled him into the vessel. Then they cast their boat loose, to sail away, but were forced to leave behind everything they had put on the island. As they sailed away, the island sank into the ocean.

Afterwards they could see the fire they had made still

burning more than two miles off, and then Brendan explained what had happened.

'Last night God revealed this mystery to me,' said the saint; 'you were not on an island at all: you were on the back of a fish; the largest fish in the ocean. This giant fish is forever trying to make his head and tail meet, but he can't, because of his great length. His name is Jasconius.'

For three days they sailed near the island where they had just been, and reached the end of it. Then they saw, towards the west, another island, not far off, across a narrow sound. This island was very grassy, well-wooded, and full of flowers; they decided to sail to its landing-place.

When they had sailed to the southern side of this island they found a rivulet flowing into the sea, and they landed the boat there. The saint ordered them to leave the boat, and tow it up against the stream, which was only just wide enough; and so they towed it for a mile up to the source of the rivulet, while the saint sat on board.

After thinking for a while, Brendan said to them, 'Look, my brothers, God has provided a suitable place for us to stay over Easter; and even if we had no other provisions, this fountain would, I believe, serve for food as well as drink.'

Because the fountain was, in truth, a very wonderful one. Over it hung a large tree, thick but not tall, all covered with snow-white birds; so many that they hid its boughs and leaves.

When the saint saw this, he wondered why such an immense number of birds had been brought together in one place. He was so puzzled that he wept and prayed to the Lord, on his bended knees, 'Oh God, you know everything, and you reveal everything that is hidden. You can see how distressed I am: please, reveal the secret of what I see here before me. I know I don't deserve to know this: please tell me out pity.'

At that, one of the birds flew off the tree, and as he flew his wings had a tinkling sound like little bells. He flew over to the boat where the saint was seated, and, perching on the prow, he spread out his wings to show how glad he was to meet Brendan.

Then the saint, realising that his prayer had been granted, said to the bird, 'If you are a messenger from God, tell me where all these birds come from, and why they are gathered together here.'

The bird answered, 'We are victims of the ancient enemy. Through no fault of our own, we fell from heaven with Lucifer and his followers. But God, who always dispenses justice, sent us to this place, where we suffer no pain, and where we can see a little of the divine presence. But we must be kept apart from the angels who remained faithful to God.

'We wander the world, in the air, and earth, and sky, like the other spirits on their missions; but on festival days we take the shapes you see, and come here, and sing the praises of our Creator. You and your brothers have now been on your voyage for one year, and you will journey for another six years. Every year, you will celebrate Easter where you celebrated it this year, until you find what your hearts long for, the Land of the Promise of the Saints.'

When he had said all this, the bird flew up from the prow of the boat, and went back to join the other birds.

As vespers approached, all the birds, in unison, clapping their wings, began to sing a hymn: 'O Lord, becometh You in Zion, and a vow shall be paid to You in Jerusalem.' They chanted the same psalm for an hour; and the melody of their warbling and the clapping of their wings sounded sweet and harmonious.

Then St Brendan said to the brothers, 'Eat and drink now, because the Lord has fed your souls full with the joys of His divine resurrection.'

When supper was ended, and Mass performed, the saint and his companions slept until midnight, when he woke them all by chanting the verse; 'You, O Lord, will open my lips.'

At that, all the birds warbled; 'Praise the Lord, all His angels, praise Him all His virtues.' And so they sang for an hour every night; and when morning dawned, they chanted; 'May the splendour of the Lord God be upon us;' in the same melody and rhythm as their morning praise of God.

At nine in the morning they sang the verse; 'Sing to our God, sing; sing to our King, sing wisely;' at noon: 'The Lord has caused the light of His face to shine upon us, and may He have mercy on us;' and at three in the afternoon they sang; 'Behold how good and how pleasant it is for brothers to dwell in unity.'

In this way, the birds gave praise to God both day and night. St Brendan, seeing all this, thanked the Lord for all His wonderful works; and the brothers fed on this spiritual food until eight days after Easter.

Brendan remained where he was with his brothers until Pentecost, listening to the delightful singing of the birds.

On the feast of Pentecost, after Brendan and the priests had celebrated Mass, their venerable provider brought enough food for the festival; and when they had sat down together to eat, he said to them, 'My brothers, you still have a long journey ahead of you. You should take vessels full of water from this fountain, and dry bread, which should keep fresh for another year, and I will supply as much as your boat can carry.'

Then he left with a blessing from all of them; and eight days later Brendan got the boat loaded up with the provisions brought by this man, together with all the vessels filled with water from the fountain.

When they had brought everything down to the shore, the bird who had spoken to them flew towards them, and landed on the prow of the boat. The saint knew that it wanted to tell him something, so he stood still where he was. Then the bird, in a human voice, said, 'You have celebrated Easter with us this year; you will also celebrate it with us next year, and next year you will celebrate Maundy Thursday at the same place where you celebrated it this year. In the same way, you will celebrate the festival of the Lord's Passover as you did before, on the back of the great fish Jasconius.

'And after eight months you will find the island of St Ailbe, where you will celebrate Christmas.'

Having made all these predictions, the bird returned to his place on the tree. The brothers got the boat ready, and set sail out into the ocean, while all the birds sang together, 'Hear us, O God our Saviour, the hope of all the ends of the earth, and in the sea afar off.'

After this, Brendan and his monks were tossed about on the billows of the ocean for three months, during which time they could see nothing but sea and sky, and they ate only every second day.

One day, however, an island came into view, not far off; but whenever they drew near the shore the wind drove them to one side, and so for forty days they sailed round and round the island without finding a landing-place.

The monks cried and prayed to the Lord to help them, because they were almost exhausted. When they had prayed like this for three days, and also fasted, they found a narrow creek just large enough for one boat, and beside it two fountains, one foul and the other clear as crystal. The brothers wasted no time trying to get to the water, but Brendan said to them, 'My children, don't do anything that may be unlawful. Don't take anything from this island without permission from the venerable fathers who live here.'

They landed, and tried to decide where they should go on the island. An old man came to them, who was so old that his body had wasted away. His hair was as white as snow, and his face was as clear as glass.

He stretched himself out on the grass three times in front of Brendan, who helped him back up and embraced him. Then all the monks gave him a hug.

Then the old man took Brendan by the hand and led him to a nearby monastery. St Brendan stood at the entrance and asked his guide whose monastery this was, and who was its abbot. He also asked him several other questions, but could get no reply: the old man just gestured with his hands. The saint soon realised that silence was the rule of the place, and he warned his brothers to keep quiet, 'Otherwise the monks here will be shocked by your silly talk, and think you are idiots.'

After this, eleven monks came out, in their habits, wearing crosses round their necks, chanting, 'Rise up, you holy ones from your dwellings, and come forth to meet us;

sanctify this place; bless this people, and vouchsafe to guard us, thy servants, in peace.'

When the monks of the island had finished their chanting, the abbot embraced St Brendan and his companions, then his monks embraced Brendan's monks. When everyone had given and received the kiss of peace, Brendan and his brothers were led into the monastery, where their feet were washed in the traditional way.

The abbot led them all into the refectory, in strict silence; and when they had washed their hands, he gave them a signal to take their seats. One of the monks, on a given signal, rose up and served them all with loaves of bread of marvellous whiteness, and delicious vegetables.

The monks had taken places at table alternately with their guests, and between each pair a whole loaf was served. The monk who was serving the food also gave them drinks.

The cheerful abbot said to his guests, 'Brothers, at this table the water from the clear fountain that you saw this morning is making a loving cup in gladness before God. We use the water of the other fountain to wash our feet, because that water is always tepid.

'We don't know where the loaves of bread which you now see before you actually come from. All we know is that some obedient creature of God brings them to our cellar, and leaves them there out of charity. For us, this proves the divine truth that "Those who fear God want for nothing."

'There are twenty-four of us here, and each day twelve loaves appear, one loaf for two brothers. On Sundays and great festivals the Lord allows us a full loaf each, so that we can make a supper with the leftovers. Because you are here, we have a double supply. This has been going on for eighty years, since the days of St Patrick and St Ailbe, our patriarchs.

'What is more, we never grow old or ill, and we don't need hot meals. We never suffer from excessive cold or heat, but we live here, as it were, in the paradise of God.

'When the times for the divine office and for Mass arrive, the lamps in our church, which, under God's guidance, we brought with us from our own country, glow into light and burn steadily.'

When the meal was over, and they had all had a drink, the abbot gave the usual signal, and all the brothers, in great silence, rose from the table, giving thanks to God. They made their way into the church, the holy fathers following on behind, where they met twelve more monks, who bowed to them as they passed.

Brendan asked, 'Father abbot, why have those monks not dined with us?'

'Our table could not seat all of us together,' the abbot explained; 'they will take their meal now, and thanks to God, they will want for nothing. Now we will enter the church and sing vespers, so that the brothers who are now dining may sing the office afterwards, in proper time.'

When vespers was finished, Brendan had a good look at the inside of the church. It was a perfect square of equal length and breadth, and in it were seven lamps, arranged so that three of them hung before the central altar, and two before each of the side altars. All the altars were made of crystal, and the chalices, patens, cruets and the other vessels used in the Mass were also of crystal.

Twenty-four benches were arranged around the church, with the abbot's seat between the two choirs of monks in rows on either side. No monk from either choir was allowed to intone the chant of the office; only the abbot; and throughout the monastery no other voice was heard, nor any other sound. If a brother needed anything, he went to the abbot, and on his knees made signs to indicate what he wanted. The abbot then wrote on a tablet what God had told him the brother wanted.

While Brendan was thinking about all these things, the abbot said to him, 'Father, it is now time to return to the refectory: we must get everything done during the daylight hours, as it is written, "He who walks in the light, won't stumble." So, when everything was finished, the monks hurried along to compline.

Then the abbot chanted the verse, 'Make us ready for your help, O Lord,' naming the Most Holy Trinity at the same time; and the rest of the monks replied, 'We have sinned; we have acted wrongly, we have done evil; You, O Lord Christ, Who are made of mercy, have pity on us.'

They went on to chant the office of compline. When the office was finished, the monks went to their cells, taking their guests with them; but the abbot remained with St Brendan in the church, waiting for the lighting of the lamps.

The saint asked the abbot about their rule of silence: how such a thing was possible in a community made up of flesh and blood people. The abbot, with much reverence and humility, replied, 'Holy father, I swear to you that during the eighty years since we came to this island, none of us has heard the sound of a human voice, unless it was singing the praises of God.

'Amongst us twenty-four brothers, no speech is used, but signs are made by the fingers or the eyes; and even this is only permitted to the older monks. And none of us, since we came here, have suffered any illness of body or mind, such as would surely shorten the life of most men.'

At this, Brendan said, with many tears, 'Tell me, I beg you, father abbot, whether we can stay here.'

The abbot replied, 'That cannot happen: it is not the will of God; but why do you ask me, when God revealed to you, before you came to us, what you must do? You must return to your own country, where God has prepared for fifteen of you the places where you will lie when you are dead. As for the other two monks, one of them will have his pilgrimage in the island of the anchorites; but the other will suffer the worst of all deaths, in hell.' And it turned out that the abbot's prophecies were all correct.

While Brendan and the abbot were talking in the church, they saw a fiery arrow passing in through a window. It flew from lamp to lamp, lighting all of them, then passed out through the same window. Brendan asked who would put out the lamps in the morning, and the abbot replied, 'Come with me, I will show you the secret of all this. Do you see those tapers burning in the vases? Notice that, though they all burn, none of them burns away, or grows less. And no ashes remain in the morning; because the light is entirely spiritual.'

'How,' asked Brendan, 'can a spiritual flame burn a real thing?'

'Have you not read,' said the abbot, 'of the burning bush near Mount Sinai, which remained intact, though it was burning?'

'Yes,' said the saint, 'I have read about it; but how is that relevant?'

They remained in the church until morning, when Brendan asked permission to leave the island. The abbot replied, 'No, O man of God, you must celebrate Christmas with us, and delight us with your company until eight days after Epiphany.' And so the holy father and his monks remained on the Island of St Ailbe until that time.

When Christmas had passed, Brendan set sail into the ocean, with the blessing of the abbot and all his monks, and with a supply of provisions. There their boat, which they did not attempt to sail or row, drifted about in various directions, until the beginning of Lent.

One day they saw an island not far off, and quickly made sail towards it. By this time they were troubled with hunger and thirst, because they had exhausted their store of food and water three days before. When Brendan had blessed the landing-place, and they had all climbed onto the shore, they found a spring of clear water, and herbs and vegetables of various kinds around it, and many sorts of fish in the stream that flowed from it to the sea.

St Brendan said, 'Brothers, God has surely given us comfort, after our weary labours. Take enough of those fish to make a meal, and cook them. Also, gather the herbs and vegetables which God has provided for His servants.'

When they had done this, they poured out some of the water to drink; but the man of God warned them: 'Brothers, make sure that you don't use too much of this water.' But the monks ignored the saint's words: some drank only one cup; but others drank two cups, and some even drank three.

The result was that some of them lapsed into a deep coma for three days and nights, though others only slept for one day and night.

St Brendan prayed to God for them for the whole time they were asleep, because he knew it was only their ignorance that had brought this sleep upon them.

After three days, Brendan said to his companions: 'Children, let us get away from this fatal place as fast as we can, and avoid any more disasters. The Lord gave you refreshment, but you overdid it, and it turned out badly for you. Before we go, we should take as much fish as we will need to make a meal on every third day, until the festival of the Lord's Supper. We should also take one cup of this water for each man, and some vegetables.'

Having loaded the boat with these provisions, they set sail into the ocean, heading north.

After three days and nights they were becalmed, and the sea became thick and curdled. The holy father said, 'Ship your oars, and loosen the sails: the Lord will guide our boat.' And so the boat sailed on for about twenty days, until God sent a good wind; then they put up their sails and rowed east, only eating every third day.

One day they saw an island that looked like a cloud, a long way off. Brendan asked the monks whether they recognised it. They said they did not, and the saint said to them: 'I know it well, my children, for we were on it last year, on the festival of the Lord's Supper. That is where our good provider lives.'

At this the monks rowed vigorously, joyfully using all their strength; but the saint said to them, 'You are foolish to wear yourselves out like this! God is the pilot of our vessel. Leave her in His hands, and He will guide her.'

When they drew near to the island, their provider came out to meet them. He praised God, then led them to the same landing-place where they had landed the year before. There he embraced the feet of Brendan and all the brothers, saying, 'God's saints are wonderful.'

Once everything had been taken out of the boat, he set up a tent, and prepared a bath for them, because it was the festival of the Lord's Supper. He also gave them all new clothes, and helped them in various other ways. Then the monks celebrated Good Friday; and when Holy Saturday was over, their provider said, 'Go back to your boat, so that you can celebrate the vigil of Easter where you celebrated it last year. There you will also celebrate the day itself, until noon.

'Then you must sail on to the Paradise of Birds, where you were last year, from Easter until the Octave of Pentecost. Take with you all the food and drink you need, and I will visit you next Sunday week.'

The monks did as he said, and Brendan set off with all his brothers, and made sail to another island.

When they drew near to the landing-place they found the cauldron that they had left on the back of Jasconius. Then Brendan set foot on the shore, and sang the Hymn of the Three Children all the way through.

He warned the monks to, 'Watch and pray, and do not be tempted. Don't forget how God put us on the back of the greatest monster in the sea, and none of us was hurt.'

The brothers kept vigil in various parts of the island, until morning, when all the monks who were also priests said their masses until nine in the morning. Then Brendan, getting into the boat with the other monks, offered to God the holy sacrifice of the Immaculate Lamb, saying, 'Last year we celebrated our Lord's Resurrection here; and I hope to celebrate it here this year as well.'

Soon they reached the Paradise of Birds again, and

when they reached the landing-place, all the birds sang, 'Salvation to our God, who sits on His throne, and to the Lamb.' Then they sang, 'The Lord is God, and He has shone upon us; appoint a solemn day, with shady boughs, even to the horn of the altar.'

That's how they warbled with the sound of their voices and their wings, until Brendan and his companions were settled in their tent. There they stayed through Easter, until the Octave of Pentecost.

Their provider came to them again on Low Sunday, as he had promised, bringing food and drink; and they all gave thanks to God.

When they were sitting down to dinner, the bird who had spoken to them before perched on the prow of the boat, clapping his wings with a loud sound, like a great organ. Brendan knew that he wanted to speak again, and sure enough he said, 'God has prepared four special places for you, for four different seasons of the year, until the seven years of your pilgrimage have ended.

'On the festival of our Lord's Supper you will be with your provider; at Easter you will be on the back of the great fish; and you will spend the Paschal time with us here, until the Octave of Pentecost. From Christmas until the festival of the Purification of the Blessed Virgin Mary you will be on the island of St Ailbe.

'After those seven years, and when you have met with many dangerous adventures, you will find the Land of the Promise of the Saints, and there you will live for forty days. Then God will guide you back to the land of your birth.'

When Brendan heard this, he wept and threw himself on the ground, as did all the monks, giving thanks and praises to the great Creator of all things. The bird then flew back to his place on the tree, and when the meal was over, their provider said, 'With God's help, I will come to you again on Pentecost Sunday with provisions.' And with a blessing from them all, he went away, and came back on the Octave of Pentecost.

Brendan stayed there, as he had been told to, and then ordered the monks to prepare the boat, and to fill all their water vessels from the fountain. When the boat was launched, their provider met them in his boat, which was full of provisions, which he quickly transferred into the boat of the man of God. With a parting embrace, he returned to wherever he had come from.

The saint sailed out into the ocean, and the boat was blown along for forty days. One day an enormous fish was spotted swimming after the boat, spouting foam from its nostrils. It was ploughing through the waves, trying to get to them, to eat them.

The monks cried out, 'O Lord, Who has made us, save us, Your servants!' They cried to Brendan, 'Help, father, help us!' The saint prayed to the Lord to deliver His servants from the belly of the monster. He also tried to comfort his fellow-monks by saying, 'Don't be afraid! God, who is always our protector, will save us from the jaws of this fish, and from every other danger.'

When the monster was getting closer, huge waves rushed on in front of it, and lapped against the gunwale of the boat, which terrified the monks; but Brendan raised up his hands to heaven and prayed, 'Oh Lord, save Your servants, just as You saved David from the giant Goliath, and Jonah from the power of the whale.'

When Brendan had finished these prayers, another

monster came from the west and attacked the first one. Then Brendan said:, 'You see, my children, the wonderful work of our Saviour; see how the creature has obeyed its Creator. This battle will bring no evil to us, but only greater glory to God.'

Then the monster that had chased the servants of God was killed, and the monster from the west bit it right through in two places, so that it was divided into three parts, right in front of all the monks, before the victorious monster swam away.

Next day they spied a wide, green island. When they drew near it, and were about to land, they found the tail of the monster that had been killed the day before.

'Look at this,' said Brendan; 'the creature that tried to devour us all. We should eat it ourselves, and fill ourselves up with it, because we will be on this island for a long time. Pull the boat higher up on the land, and look for a good place to pitch our tent.'

But it was Brendan himself who found a place, and the monks set up the tent. 'Take enough meat from this monster to feed us for three months,' said Brendan, 'because tonight the rest of it will be eaten by the fishes of the sea.'

And so the brothers saved as much meat as was needed; but then asked Brendan, 'Holy father, how can we live here without water to drink?'

'Is it more difficult,' asked the saint, 'for the Almighty to give us water than to give us food? Go to the southern side of the island, and there you will find a spring of clear water, as well as plenty of herbs and vegetables. Take all you need.'

They went, and found everything just as the man of

God had told them.

Brendan remained on this island for three months, because there were violent storms in the sea all round, as well as hail and rain. The monks went to see what had become of the remains of the monster, and they found, where its carcass had been, only its bones, as their father had predicted.

When they mentioned this to him he said, 'If you feel you need to test the truth of my words, I will give you another sign; tonight a large section of a fish will break loose from a fisherman's net, and will wash up here, on our beach. And that will be tomorrow's dinner.'

Next day the monks went to the place Brendan said the fish would be, and found exactly what the man of God had predicted. They rolled up their sleeves, and brought away as much fish as they could carry.

Then venerable father said to them, 'Keep this carefully, and salt it, because we will need it very badly. The Lord will grant calm weather today and tomorrow; and on the third day, when the storms have died down, we will leave this island.'

When the time came, Brendan ordered them to load their boat with the skins and water-vessels filled from the fountain, and also enough herbs and vegetables to last them. (The saint, since he had become a priest, had never eaten meat.) With the boat properly stocked, they set off due north.

One day they saw an island far off, and Brendan said to his brothers, 'On that island there are three classes of people: boys, young men, and old men. Now, one of our brothers will have his pilgrimage there.'

The monks asked him which of them it was, but he was reluctant to name him. But when they pressed the question, and seemed upset because he would not answer them, he pointed and said, 'This is the brother who will stay on this island.'

He was one of the monks who had come after the saint from his own monastery: and Brendan had made a prediction about him when they set off. Then they drew near to the island, and the boat touched the shore.

The island was amazingly flat, almost level with the sea itself, and there were no trees, or anything that waved in the wind. It was a big island, covered all over with white and purple flowers.

Here, as the man of God had said, there were three troops of monks, standing apart, about a stone's throw from each other, and keeping at this distance when they moved in any direction. One choir chanted, 'The saints will go from goodness to goodness; God will be seen in Zion;' and then another choir took up the same chant; and in this way, they chanted without stopping. The first choir was of boys in snow-white robes; the second was of young men, dressed in violet; and the third was the old men, in purple robes.

When the boat reached the landing-place it was noon; and at two o'clock all the choirs of monks together sang the psalm, 'May God have mercy on us, and bless us, to the end,' and 'come to my aid, O Lord;' and also the psalm, 'I have believed, and I have spoken,' with the proper prayer.

At three o'clock they chanted three other psalms in the same way; 'Out of the depths I have cried to you, O Lord;' 'Behold how good and how pleasant it is for brothers to live together in unity;' and 'Praise the Lord, O Jerusalem;

praise your God, O Zion.'

Again, at Vespers, they sang the psalms: 'A hymn, O Lord, is for you in Zion;' 'Bless the Lord, O my soul;' and 'Praise the Lord, children; praise the name of the Lord;' Then they chanted, sitting down, the fifteen gradual psalms [Psalms 120-134].

After they had finished this chanting, a bright, glowing cloud cast its shadow over the island, so that they could not see anything; but they heard the monk's voices chanting in the same way until morning, when they sung the psalms; 'Praise the Lord from the heavens; sing unto the Lord;' and 'Praise the Lord in his saints;' and then twelve psalms, in the order of the psaltery, as far as the psalm; 'The fool says in his heart'.

At dawn, the cloud passed away from the island, and then the choirs chanted the three psalms: 'Have mercy on me, O Lord; the Lord is my refuge;' and, 'O God, my God'.

At nine, they sang three other psalms; 'Oh, clap your hands, all you nations;' 'Save me, O God, by Your name;' and, 'I have loved, because the Lord will hear the voice of my prayer,' with the Alleluia. Then they celebrated Mass, and they all received the Holy Communion with the words, 'This Sacred Body of the Lord and the Blood of our Saviour receive unto life everlasting.'

When Mass was finished, two members of the choir of young men brought a basket full of purple grapes, and put it into the man of God's boat, saying, 'Eat the fruit of the isle of the Strong Men, and give us the brother you have chosen; then go in peace.'

Brendan then called this brother to him, and said, 'Give the kiss of peace to your brothers, and go with those who have invited you. I say to you, your mother conceived you in a happy hour: you deserve to live with such a holy community.'

Brendan then gave him the kiss of peace, with many tears, and so did the other monks. Brendan said to him, 'Remember, my dear son, the special favours God has shown you; go, and pray for us.'

Bidding them all farewell, the brother quickly followed the two young men to the company of the saints, who sang the verse, 'Behold how good and pleasant it is for brothers to dwell together in unity,' as soon as they saw him. In a higher key, they chanted, 'We praise You, O God;' and then, when they had all embraced him, he became one of them.

Brendan set sail, and, when meal-time came, he told the monks to eat the grapes from the island. He picked up one of the grapes and saw how big and juicy it was: 'I have never seen or even read about such large grapes,' he said. They were all the same size and shape, like large balls, and when the juice of one was squeezed into a cup, it weighed a whole pound. Brendan divided the juice into twelve portions, and gave one portion a day to each of the monks. In this way one grape proved to be enough for all of them; and the juice itself tasted like honey.

Later, Brendan ordered a three days' fast, after which a resplendent bird flew towards the boat, carrying in its beak a branch from an unknown tree. On the branch there was a cluster of very red grapes: the bird dropped it near the man of God, and flew away. 'Enjoy this feast that the Lord has sent us,' said Brendan. The grapes were as big as apples, and he gave some to each of the monks. So they had food enough for four days, after which they went back to fasting.

After three days they saw an island covered all over with trees, set close together, and full of grapes like those they had last eaten. There were so many grapes on each tree that all the branches were weighed down to the ground; there were no fruitless trees, or trees with other types of fruit, on the whole island.

The monks drew up to the landing-place, and Brendan left the boat and walked around the island, where the fragrance was like that of a house full of pomegranates. Meanwhile his brothers remained in the boat, waiting for his return, and the fragrant wind from the island blew towards them, and made them feel hungry.

Brendan found six fountains on the island, watering the green herbs, and vegetables of many kinds. He then returned to his brothers, bringing with him some samples, and he said to them, 'Leave the boat now, and fix up our tent here; be of good cheer, and enjoy the excellent fruits of this land, which God has shown to us.' And so for forty days they feasted on the grapes, herbs and vegetables that were watered by the fountains.

Soon they embarked again, taking with them some of the fruits of the island, and sailed along, letting the winds dictate their course.

Suddenly there appeared flying towards them a type of bird called a griffon. When the monks saw it, they cried out to the holy father, 'Help us! This monster has come to devour us.' But the man of God told them not to fear it, because God was their helper.

Soon another great bird came into view, and flew against the griffon. The two creatures fought for a long time, and it was hard to tell which of them would win, but when the second griffon tore out the eyes of the first, it was beaten, and fell, dead, into the sea, while the monks looked on. At this, the brothers gave thanks, and the victorious bird flew away.

Next, they went to the island of St Ailbe, to celebrate Christmas. There, after taking leave of the abbot, with mutual blessings, they sailed about in the ocean for a long time, taking rest only at Easter and Christmas on the the islands mentioned before.

Once, when Brendan was celebrating the festival of St Peter in the boat, they found that the sea was so clear, they could easily see what was at the bottom. They saw beneath them various monsters of the deep, and so clear was the water, that it seemed as if they could touch the bottom of the deep sea with their hands. The fishes were visible in great shoals, like flocks of sheep in their pastures, swimming around, heads to tails.

The monks begged the man of God to say Mass in a low voice, in case those monsters of the deep, hearing the strange sound, might be stirred up to attack them; but the saint said, 'I am amazed at your foolishness. Why do you dread those monsters? Is not the largest of them already dead? How can you forget that you have chopped wood, and made a fire on his back, and even cooked some of it? Why should you fear the monsters down below us? Our God is the Lord Jesus Christ, who can bring all living things to destruction.'

When he had said this, Brendan sang the Mass in a louder voice than usual, as the monks carried on gazing at the large fishes below them. When these creatures heard the voice of the man of God, they rose up from the depths, and swam around the boat in such numbers, that the monks could see nothing but the swimming fishes. These did not come too close to the boat, but swam around at some distance, until the Mass was ended. Then they swam away in different directions, until the monks couldn't see them any more.

This strange, clear, pellucid sea was so vast that even with a favourable wind, and all sails set, they were scarcely able to pass out of it in eight days.

One day, on which three Masses had been said, they saw a column in the sea, which seemed not far off, yet they could not reach it for three days. When they drew near it Brendan looked towards its summit, but could not see it, because of its great height. It was so tall, it seemed to pierce the sky. It was covered over with a canopy, made of an unknown material that had the colour of silver and was as hard as marble. The column itself was made of the clearest crystal.

Brendan ordered the monks to take in their oars, and to lower the sails and mast; then he ordered some of them to hold onto the fringes of the canopy, which ended about a mile from the column, and stretched down into the sea for about a mile as well. When this had been done, Brendan said, 'Run the boat in through an opening, so that we can get a closer look at the wonderful works of God.'

When they had passed through the opening, and looked around them, the sea seemed transparent like glass. They could plainly see everything beneath them, even the base of the column, and the skirts of the canopy lying on the ground, because the sun shone just as brightly inside as outside. Brendan measured an opening between four pavilions, and found them to be four cubits on every side.

When they sailed for a whole day along one side of the column, they could always feel the shade as well as the heat of the sun, beyond three o'clock in the afternoon; and after sailing around the column for four days, they found each side to be four hundred cubits long.

On the fourth day, they discovered a chalice and a dish on the south side. The chalice was made of the same material as the canopy, and the dish was made of crystal, like the column. Brendan took up these things and said, 'The Lord Jesus Christ has displayed this great marvel to us, and has given us two miraculous gifts, which we can show to the world.'

The holy father then directed the monks to perform the divine office, and afterwards to eat and drink, which they hadn't done since they had came in sight of the column.

Next day they rowed towards the north, and having passed out through an opening, they set up the mast, and unfurled the sails again, while some of them held on by the fringes of the canopy, until the boat was ready. When they set sail, a favourable wind came on behind them, so that they didn't need to row. All they had to do was to hold the ropes and the tiller. In this way, they travelled north.

After eight days they came within view of an island which was very rugged and rocky, and covered over with slag. There were no trees or other plants, but the island was full of blacksmiths' forges. Brendan said to his brothers, 'I have a bad feeling about this island. I have no wish to go ashore, or even approach it, but the wind is driving us directly towards it, as if we are supposed to go there.'

When they were about a stone's throw from the shore, they heard the noise of bellows blowing like thunder, and the beating of hammers on anvils. Brendan armed himself with the sign of the Cross, and said, 'O Lord Jesus Christ, deliver us from this evil island.'

Soon, one of the inhabitants came out to do some work. He was all hairy and hideous, his skin blackened and grimy from fire and smoke. When he saw the servants of Christ near the island, he went back into his forge, crying out, 'Woe! Woe! Woe!'

Brendan crossed himself again, and said to the monks, 'Put on more sail, and row more briskly, so that we can get away from here.'

Hearing this, the savage man rushed down to the shore, carrying tongs with a burning piece of slag gripped in them. The slag was large and very hot, and he threw it after the servants of Christ; but it didn't hurt them, because they were protected by the sign of the Cross.

It missed them by a good furlong, and where it fell into the sea, it fumed up like a heap of burning coals, pushing out smoke like a fiery furnace. When they had sailed about a mile beyond the spot where this burning mass had fallen, all the natives of the island crowded down to the shore, each carrying a huge piece of burning slag. One at a time, each of them threw his burning slag after the servants of God. Then they returned to their forges, which they blew up into mighty flames, so that the whole island seemed like a giant globe of fire, and the sea on every side boiled up and foamed, like a cauldron set on a fire well-supplied with fuel.

All day the brothers heard a loud wailing from the inhabitants of the island, even when they could no longer see it; and they could smell a nasty stench, even when they were miles away.

Brendan then tried to summon up the courage of the brothers, by saying, 'Soldiers of Christ, be strong in true faith and in the armour of the Spirit, because we are now on the very edge of hell. Be watchful, and behave like men.'

On another day they spotted a huge mountain in the sea, not far off, towards the north. The mountain had misty clouds all around it, and masses of smoke pouring out of its summit.

Suddenly the wind drove the boat rapidly towards the island until it almost touched the shore. The cliffs were so high that they could hardly see the top of them. They were as black as coal, and as steep as a wall. Here the one monk who was still with them, out of the three who had followed Brendan from his monastery, leaped out of the boat. He made his way to the foot of the cliff, wailing and crying aloud, 'Woe is me! Father: I am torn away from you by force! I cannot return.'

The other monks, terrified, quickly rowed off from the shore and cried out to the Lord, 'Have mercy on us, have mercy on us!'

Brendan saw plainly how the wretched monk on the shore was carried off by a whole swarm of demons, and how his body was already on fire. The saint cried out, 'Misery is yours, unhappy man; misery has made an evil end to your life.'

Later, a favourable breeze caught the boat, and drove them southwards. As they looked back, they saw that the peak of the mountain was no longer covered with clouds. It was shooting up flames into the sky, then sucking them back into itself, so that it seemed like a burning pyre.

After this dreadful sight, they sailed for seven days towards the south, and then Brendan spotted a very thick cloud. As they got nearer to the cloud, they saw the shape of a man, sitting on a rock, with a veil in front of him as large as a sack, hanging between two iron prongs. The man was tossed about like a small boat in a storm. When the monks saw this, some of them thought it was a bird, and others thought it was a boat. The man of God told them to stop arguing about this, and to steer directly for the place.

When they arrived, they found that the waves all around were motionless, as if they had frozen over. They found the man sitting on a rugged and shapeless rock, with the waves on every side. As they flowed, the waves battered him from head to toe, and the cloth which hung in front of him struck him on the eyes and on the forehead.

The saint asked him who he was, why he was there, and what crime he had committed, which meant that he deserved to suffer such a terrible punishment.

He answered, 'I am Judas, the most miserable of men, and the most wicked. Through the mercy of Jesus Christ, I am placed here every year, on the anniversary of His resurrection. While I sit here, I seem to myself to be in a paradise of delights, considering the agony of the torments that are in store for me afterwards. When I am in my torments, I burn like a mass of molten lead, day and night, in the heart of that mountain that you have seen.

'Leviathan and his followers live there, and I was there when the mountain swallowed down your lost brother. All hell rejoiced at that, and belched out great flames, as it always does, when it devours the souls of the wicked.

'I have this refreshing coolness every Sunday from the first vespers to the second; from Christmas Day to the

Epiphany; from Easter to Pentecost; on the Purification of the Blessed Virgin Mary; and on the festival of her Assumption. On all other days I am in torments with Herod and Pilate, and with Annas and Caiaphas.

'I beg you, in the name of the Redeemer of the world, to pray for me to the Lord Jesus. Ask him to let me remain here until sunrise tomorrow, and to keep off the demons, and stop them dragging me to hell too soon.'

Then the saint said, 'The will of the Lord be done; you will not be taken away by the demons until tomorrow.' And he asked him about the cloth that fluttered in front of him.

Judas replied, 'I once gave this cloth to a leper, when I was the purse-bearer of the Lord; but as it was not my own, it hurts me, and doesn't help me. I once gave the iron prongs it hangs on to the priests to support their cauldrons; and the stone on which I sit, I placed in a trench on a public road before I became a disciple of the Lord's.'

When evening came, a great swarm of demons gathered around in a circle, shouting to Brendan, 'Go away, O man of God! We cannot come near our comrade unless you go away, and we dare not look at the devil again until we bring his pet victim back to him. So give us our prey, and don't keep him from us tonight.'

'I'm not protecting him,' said the saint, 'but the Lord Jesus Christ allows him to stay here tonight.'

The demons cried out, 'How could you use the name of the Lord to help the man who betrayed Him?'

Then the man of God commanded them, in the name of Jesus Christ, not to touch him till morning.

At dawn, when Brendan was about to leave Judas, a countless swarm of demons covered the sea, crying out,

'O man of God, we curse your coming and going. Tonight Lucifer has scourged us until we have deep scars on our backs, because we did not bring back his wretched captive.'

'Those curses will fall on yourselves, not on us,' said the saint, 'because the man you curse is blessed, and the creature you bless is cursed.'

The demons shouted, 'He will suffer double punishment for the next six days, because you saved him from his punishment last night.' But the man of God warned them, 'You and your chief have no power except the power God gives you; and I command you in the name of the Lord, not to increase his torments.'

'Are you God?' they asked, 'that you expect us to obey your command?'

'No,' the saint replied, 'but I am the servant of the Lord; and whatever I command in His name, it is done, and I am His minister only in what He grants to me.'

In this way they pursued Brendan with their blasphemies until he was far away from Judas; then they carried off his wretched soul with great rushing and howling.

After this, Brendan made sail for some time towards the south, giving the glory to God. On the third day, a small island appeared at a distance, and the monks rowed towards it, but Brendan said to them, 'Brothers, don't exhaust yourselves! Next Easter, it will be seven years since we left our country, and now on this island we will see a holy hermit, called Paul the Spiritual, who has lived there for sixty years. For all those years he has never eaten any food, and for twenty years before that, all the food he ate came from a certain animal.'

When they drew near the shore, they could find no place to land, because the coast was so steep. The island was small and circular, about two hundred yards in circumference, and on its summit there was no soil, the rock being quite bare.

When they sailed around it, they found a small creek, hardly big enough for the prow of their boat. The sides of the creek were also steep, and hard to climb. Brendan told the brothers to wait there until he came back to them, because he knew they shouldn't set foot on the island, until the man of God who lived there had given them permission.

Brendan climbed right up to the top of the island and saw, on its eastern side, two caves opening opposite each other. There was also a small cup-like spring of water gurgling up from the rock, at the mouth of one of the caves. As Brendan approached the opening of one of the caves, a venerable hermit came out to greet him, saying, 'Look how good and how pleasant it is for brothers to live together in unity.'

And then he directed St Brendan to summon all the other monks from the boat. When they came, he gave each of them the kiss of peace, calling each by his proper name. They were all very surprised by this, because the old man seemed to speak like a prophet. They were also amazed by his clothing, because he was covered all over from head to foot with his own hair, which was as white as snow from old age: this was the only outfit he wore.

Brendan was sad when he looked at the old man, and he said, 'Pity me: I am a poor sinner, who wears a monk's habit, and rules over many monks, but here I see a man like an angel, living without any of the temptations of life.'

The old man replied, saying, 'Venerable father, what great and wonderful things God has shown to you: things that were not seen by any of the saints who went before you. And yet, you say that you are not worthy to wear the habit of a monk? I say to you, that you are greater than any monk!

'Monks are fed and clothed by the labour of their own hands, but God has fed and clothed you and all your brothers for seven years in His own mysterious ways! And I, wretch that I am, sit here on this rock, without any covering except the hair of my own body.'

Then Brendan asked him how he had come to the island, where he came from, and how long be had lived there. The man of God replied, 'For forty years I lived in the monastery of St Patrick, where I looked after the cemetery. One day, the prior pointed out to me the place where one of the monks should be buried; but an old man, whom I had never seen before, appeared to me. He said, "Brother, do not dig that grave there; that is the burial-place for someone else." I said, "Who are you, father?"

' "Don't you know me?" he asked; "am I not your abbot?"

' "St Patrick is my abbot," I said.

' "I am Patrick," he said, "but yesterday I died, and this is my burial-place."

'Then he pointed out another place to me, saying, "Here you should bury our dead brother, but don't tell anyone what I have said to you. Tomorrow, go down to the shore, and there you will find a boat that will carry you to the place where you will wait for the day of your death."

'Next morning I went down to the shore, and found

exactly what Patrick had promised. I got into the boat, and rowed along for three days and nights. After that, I allowed the boat to drift wherever the wind drove it. On the seventh day, this rock appeared. I landed, and pushed off the boat with my foot, and it returned to where it had come from, cutting through the waves at an amazing speed.

'When I arrived here, a certain animal, walking on its hind legs, brought me a fish for my dinner, and a bundle of dry brushwood to make a fire. When it had put these in front of me, it went away again.

'I used a flint and steel to start the fire, and cooked the fish. In this way, I lived for thirty years: the same animal brought me a fish every third day, so that I never went hungry. Thanks to God, every Sunday enough water flowed from the rock to allow me to slake my thirst and to wash myself.

'After thirty years I discovered these two caves and this spring. I have lived on the waters of the spring for sixty years, without any other nourishment whatsoever.

'So, altogether I have lived on this island for ninety years. When I first got here, I was already fifty years old, so that I am now one hundred and forty years old. For the rest of my life, I must wait here on this island until the Day of Judgement.

'Brendan, you must now continue your voyage. Fill your water-vessels from this fountain, because you will be at sea for forty days, until Easter Saturday. You will celebrate Easter, and all the Paschal holidays, where you have celebrated them for the past six years. After that, with a blessing from your provider, you will sail to the land that you seek, the most holy of all lands. You will live there for forty days, after which the Lord your God will guide you safely back to the land of your birth.'

When they had received the blessing of the man of God, Brendan and his monks sailed due south during Lent. All they ate or drank during this time was the water from the island, which they drank every third day. They were glad, as they felt neither hunger nor thirst. On Holy Saturday they reached the island of their provider, who came to meet them at the landing-place, and lifted every one of them out of the boat in his arms. As soon as the divine offices of the day were duly performed, he set a meal before them.

In the evening they got into their boat with this man, and soon discovered, in the usual place, the huge fish. They sang the praises of the Lord all night on the back of the fish, and said Mass in the morning. When Mass had finished, Jasconius moved away, while they were all still on his back. At this, the monks cried out to the Lord, 'Hear us, O Lord, the God of our salvation,' but Brendan calmed them down by saying, 'Why are you scared? Don't be afraid: nothing bad can happen to us! The fish is just taking us where we want to go!'

The fish swam in a direct course towards the shore of the Paradise of Birds, where it landed them all unharmed. They stayed there until the Octave of Pentecost, and when that solemn season had passed, their provider, who was still with them, said to Brendan, 'Get into your boat again, and fill all the water-skins from the fountain. I will be your pilot for the rest of your journey, because without my help you will never find the Land of the Promise of the Saints.'

As they were setting off, all the birds of the island sang, 'May a happy voyage bring you safely to the island of your provider.'

They had enough provisions for forty days, during which time they travelled east. At the end of forty days, towards evening, a dense cloud overshadowed them. It was so dark that they could hardly see one another. Then their provider asked Brendan, 'Do you know what darkness this is?' The saint replied that he didn't know. 'This darkness,' said their provider, 'surrounds the island you have looked for for seven years; in fact, it is the entrance to that island.'

After an hour, a great light shone around them, and they found that their boat stood by the shore.

This new island was very large, and thickly set with trees laden with fruits, as if it were autumn. The whole time they were in that land, there was no night, but a light always shone, like the light of the sun. They explored all over the island for forty days, but they could never find an end to it.

One day they came to a wide river flowing towards the middle of the land, which they could not cross by any means. Brendan said to the monks, 'We cannot cross over this river, so we'll never get a true idea of the size of this country.'

While they were thinking about this, a very handsome young man came to them. He joyfully embraced every one of them, and called each one by his own name. Then he said, 'Peace be with you, brothers, and with all who live in the peace of Christ. Blessed are they who live in your house, O Lord; they will praise You for ever and ever.'

Then he said to St Brendan, 'This is the land you have been looking for for all these years. You couldn't find it before now because Christ our Lord wanted to show you the many mysteries of the ocean. You should now return to the land of your birth; you should take with you as much of this fruit, and as many of these precious stones, as your boat can carry.

'The days of your earthly pilgrimage are now ending, and soon you will rest in peace among your saintly brothers. After many years this land will be made known to those who come after you, when days of trouble may come upon the people of Christ.

'The great river you see here divides this land into two parts, and this land is always just as you see it now, teeming with ripe fruits, without any blight or shadow whatever, but always in bright sunlight.'

When St Brendan asked whether this land would ever be made known to men, the young man replied, 'When the Most High Creator rules all the nations, this land will be made known to His chosen people.'

Soon after, Brendan received the blessing of this man, and prepared for his return to his own country. He gathered some of the fruits of the island, and various kinds of precious stones. At last, having taken a last farewell of the man who had provided food for him and his brothers, he embarked once more.

When they had passed back through the darkness, they reached the Island of Delights, where they remained for three days, as guests in the monastery. Then Brendan, with the abbot's parting blessing, set sail in a direct course, under God's guidance, and arrived at his own monastery. There all his monks gave glory to God for the safe return of their holy patron. Soon he told them all about the wonderful works of God, which he had seen during his voyage.

Later he ended the days of his life in peace, on the ninth of July, our Lord Jesus Christ reigning, whose kingdom and empire endure for ever and ever. Amen!

III. Brendan After His Voyage

(From the Latin Life of St Brendan in the Codex Armachanus; in the Library of Trinity College, Dublin)

When St Brendan returned from his voyage in quest of the Land of the Promise of the Saints, he founded many religious houses all over Ireland. It was then that many people brought large offerings to Brendan, in the name of Christ. Many others gave up all their worldly possessions, and were received into the religious life by the man of God. In the end, three thousand monks were under his rule. He even made his own father a monk, and made his mother a consecrated widow.

Meanwhile the saint visited his foster-mother, St Ita, who welcomed him most tenderly, with an affectionate embrace. She was enthralled by Brendan's stories of the marvellous things he had seen on the ocean. Soon after, the saint took his departure from her, with mutual blessings.

He travelled to an island called Inis-da-dromand, which lies in a northern estuary of the lower Shannon, the river that flows between the countries of West Clare and Kerry.

There he founded a famous monastery, where, within a brief period, seven members of the community died, in the odour of sanctity, and the mortuary chapel of that place was erected over their sacred relics.

About the same time, the saint gave his blessing to

fifty streams in various districts, which had been fish-less. Thanks to the blessing of the man of God, they were soon packed with fish. In course of time he passed into the province of Connaught, where land was granted to him, on which he founded the famous city of Clonfert, in which he was buried.

Once, Brendan came to the town of Bri-uys, in the district of Cliath, near the Hill of the Swine, and stayed there overnight.

The people of the town complained to him about the terrible plague of insects they were suffering at that time. The saint prayed to Almighty God that the inhabitants of that town might be freed from these harmful pests, and as a result of his prayer the insects started to disappear, and were soon gone altogether. In fact, from that day to this, no insects can live in that town.

One day St Brendan sailed to the above-mentioned island of Inis-da-dromand, and left his boat at the shore, in the charge of a young monk. When the sea rose very high, the brother of this monk said to Brendan, 'Holy father, the tide is running very strongly, and is taking away the boat from the shore. It will soon drown my brother, and he will perish.'

But Brendan grew impatient and said, 'Do you love this brother more than I do? If you think so, and if you want to show more compassion for him than I have, go to him now, and die instead of him.'

The brother went at once to the place of danger, and suddenly the sea rose up around him on every side, and he was drowned. But the young monk, his brother, was saved, because the sea became like a wall around him, as the Red Sea had been for Moses.

Later, Brendan became frightened of the Lord, on account of the death of this monk, because he judged himself to be responsible for it, and he asked the advice of saintly men about this.

Their advice was that he should go to his foster-mother, St Ita, who was inspired by God with a prophetic spirit, and she would tell him what he ought to do. Ita advised him to go on a pilgrimage for some time, to atone for the brother's death; and to preach the Gospel elsewhere, so as to lead other souls to Christ.

Later, the venerable St Gildas said to Brendan, 'There is a wilderness not far from here, and it is full of very powerful wild beasts. They frequently attack the local people, and often come to this city of ours. Brendan, God has given you the power to expel those beasts from amongst us. If you can do this, I believe that through divine grace you will be forgiven for the fault that made you start out on your pilgrimage.'

And so Brendan went out into the wilderness, taking with him his disciple, Talmach. A number of men on horseback followed them, and looked on at a distance, eager to see what would happen.

When they came to the lair of the wild beasts, they found the mother of the beasts, with her young ones, asleep in the noonday sun. Holy Talmach went to wake her up, and she let out a loud roar. When they heard this, all the other beasts rushed towards her. Then Brendan said to her, 'Follow us now very gently, with all your cubs.'

The people who were watching from a distance expected Brendan and Talmach to be killed, but instead they saw the wild beasts following them like pet dogs. But the men on horseback still galloped away, terrified.

When Gildas saw how tame the monsters were, even at the gates of the city, he gave thanks to God for His wonderful works. Then Brendan commanded the beasts to go back again into the wilderness, and never to harm anyone any more. Nobody knows what became of them: they have not been seen since then, right up to the present day.

After this the venerable St Gildas said to Brendan, 'Accept me now, father, as a disciple of yours, and become the patron of this city and people.'

But Brendan replied, 'I must not stay here, because on the Day of Judgement, I must be resurrected in Ireland.'

Brendan received the blessings of Gildas and all his monks, as well as the blessings of the people of the city. He gave them his blessing in return, and left that place.

One day when Brendan was on his voyages on the ocean, he saw two monsters of the deep in dreadful conflict, one of them chasing the other with great fury. When the monster that was being chased was about to be overtaken and killed by the other monster, it cried out, in a human voice, 'I commend myself to the protection of St Patrick, the Chief-Bishop of the Irish.'

The other monster then shouted, 'His protection won't help you now!'

Then the first monster cried out, 'I commend myself to the protection of St Brendan here,' and then his pursuer said, 'Neither will his protection save you now.'

At last the first monster cried out, 'I commend myself to the protection of the most holy virgin Brigid.'

At that, the monster in pursuit withdrew straight away,

saying that it dare not chase another monster that had asked for the protection of Brigid. In this way, the wretched creature escaped unharmed.

After that, Brendan composed a hymn in praise of St. Brigid, for the greater glory of God; and when he returned to Ireland, he went to visit that saint. He told her about the monsters, and asked her why such monsters of the deep had more fear of her than of other saints. The holy virgin replied with a question: 'How often do you fix your attention on God?'

Brendan answered, 'At every seventh step I take, or sooner, I have God in my thoughts, but sometimes I think of God alone for a long space of time.'

Then Brigid said, 'So sometimes you think about worldly things, and at other times you think about God. For my part, since I first applied my mind to God, I have never for a moment thought of anything but Him. The more constantly you fix the attention of your mind and the love of your heart on God, the more the animals will be afraid of you.'

Brendan was deeply affected by Brigid's words, and having received her blessing, and giving his blessing in return, he went on his way.

St Brendan then came to Connaught, and went to an island called Inis-meic-Ichuind, where the king's horses were at pasture. Here the saint built an oratory, and used the king's horses as draught animals. The holy bishop Moenu was there with Brendan at the time.

When King Aedh, son of Eathach Tirmcama, heard of this, he was angry, and said that he would surely put to death the person who had done him so great a wrong. In his rage he hurried to the island, but when he was preparing to cross over to it in a boat, there was a violent storm, so that the king had to wait on the shore of the lake for three days, until it was calm. On the night of the third day the Lord appeared to the king in a dream, and said to him, 'Do no harm to My servant Brendan: if you hurt him, you will soon meet your death.' When the storm died down, the king made a gift of the island, together with the horses, to St Brendan, forever.

At about this time, Brendan sent five monks into his monastery on Inis-da-dromand so that they could remain in that community. But one day, a demon sowed strife between them, and one of them wounded another monk (who was a senior) in the head by stealth. When this brother died, some of the monks ran to Brendan, and told him what had happened.

The holy father said to them, 'Go back at once, and tell your wounded brother to wake up from his sleep: tell him his abbot, Brendan, is calling him.'

They returned and said these words to their dead brother, and he immediately rose up and went to Brendan, still carrying the iron weapon with which he was wounded, stuck in his head.

When Brendan saw him he asked, 'Dear brother, do you want to live for ever down here on the earth, or would you rather go to heaven straight away?' The brother chose to go to Christ straight away, and so he died in peace. He was buried on the island of Inisquin, and his grave there is called in Irish, Lebayd in tollcynd (the bed of the wounded head) and is regarded as a holy place.

One day Brendan went to the mainland, and he met an unhappy man there, who cried and cast himself at the saint's feet, saying, 'Take pity on me, oh holy father! I have been reduced to slavery by my lord the king!'

Brendan, seeing he was miserable, turned up the earth with his staff, and pulled out a lump of gold, which he gave to the man. He told him to tell no one, but to give this gold to the king, who would then free him and his children.

But the man did tell the king how he had got the gold, and then the king, when he heard of the miracle from him, said, 'This gold is the gift of Christ, and it is not my right, but that of His servants, to keep it. I will grant you and your children freedom for nothing: you are free to go.'

Soon, the freed man returned to Brendan with the gold he had given him, giving thanks to God for his freedom.

Brendan was seventy-seven years old when he founded his monastery and city of Clonfert ; and while he was there, a certain monk, who had come away with the saint from his parents in Britain, died in the monastery. On the third day after his death, Brendan said to the holy Bishop Moenu, 'Place my staff on the body of the dead brother.' When the bishop had laid the staff on the body, the man arose from the dead. He proved to be in perfect health, and much strengthened in faith, and he went back to Britain, his own country.

Ita, Brendan's foster-mother, said in her heart one Christmas night, 'I wish I could receive the Holy Communion from the hands of my foster-son, most holy Brendan, on this blessed night.'

When the holy virgin, full of faith, rose during the

night to celebrate the vigil of the festival in her convent, she was taken up by an angel and carried to the city of Clonfert-Brendan. There Brendan, who had foreseen her visit to him, went out to meet her in the porch of his church, carrying the Blessed Sacrament. Having landed on the earth, the saint of God received the Holy Communion from the hand of St Brendan, giving thanks to Christ.

When the saints had blessed each other, the holy virgin was carried back to her own convent by the angel. The distance from St Ita's convent, Cluaincredail, in Munster, to the city of Clonfert-Brendan in Connaught, was a three days' journey, but by angel, the return trip took just an hour.

In the district of Muscry-tire, in the province of Munster, a flame burst out from the earth, and gave off a terrible stench. The local people tried to put it out with water, but in vain. Brendan was there, and saw that the land was being burned up by the flames, which were rising higher all the time. He said to the people, 'This is a fire from hell issuing out of the earth.'

They begged him to help, and he said to them, 'Make a three days' fast, and I will pray to God for you.'

When they had fasted three days, the saint told them go to St Chiar, a holy virgin, to whom God had given the power to extinguish the fire by prayer alone. When St Chiar had prayed to God against the fire, the flames were completely extinguished, and they never appeared again.

When Brendan went to visit the saints of Meath, Diarmait MacCearbhail, who then reigned at Tara as monarch of Ireland, had a vision in a dream. In his dream, he saw two angels taking the royal collar of gold from his neck, and giving it to a man he didn't recognise.

On the following day Brendan came to visit the king, who told his courtiers that this was the man his royal collar had been given to, in his vision. Then the king's wise men told him that his vision meant that power over Ireland would now be shared, by the kings, with the saints of the country. And they said that Brendan would be a great power in the land.

One day when St Brendan was on a journey, a great storm of hail and snow came down on him and his companions. Some of the monks said to Brendan, 'Holy father, this cold is worse that the cold in hell!'

'You speak like ignorant country people,' the saint replied. 'We have seen Judas, the betrayer of our Lord, in a dreadful sea, on the Lord's day, wailing and lamenting, seated on a rugged, slimy rock. A fiery wave from the east, and an icy cold wave from the west took turns to batter the rock, which drenched Judas in a frightful manner. And yet this punishment seemed to him a relief from pain, and a break from his torments. So what must it be like in hell itself?' When the monks heard this, they begged Almighty God to take pity on their miseries.

On another day, when Brendan was travelling through a forest, a violent storm was raging, blowing down trees on every side as he and his companions travelled on. One of the monks said to the others, 'We are in great danger from these falling trees.'

Then Brendan told them, 'One night, while all our crew were asleep in the boat on the wide ocean, I alone remained awake.

'We came to an island which had many openings

through it. It was supported on four great legs over the sea, and between those legs our boat passed under the island, so that we sailed right through, while the island stood above us.

'Brothers, that shows how God, who can keep an island up in the air on legs, can save us from the danger of falling trees.'

When they heard this, the brothers grew stronger in their confidence in Christ.

Once, the King of Munster came into Connaught with a large army, to lay waste that country. Brendan was then very old, but the men of Connaught begged him to go out to meet the Munstermen, and convince them to make peace. But these men were so proud that they would not agree to peace, or even a truce.

When they carried on ravaging the country, they found themselves going round and round in a circle for a whole day, unable to break out or make any progress. They realised that a miracle had been used against them as a weapon, and, terrified, decided to return to their own country. Thus through the power of God, they went home empty-handed; for who can resist the will of the Almighty?

When Brendan was returning from these men, the people brought him a boy who was dumb from his birth. The man of God blessed his tongue, and at once the boy spoke clearly, and all the people who were present gave glory to God.

When he was very old, St Brendan went to visit his sister, St Briag, who was governing a convent of nuns at Eanachduin, under his direction.

While he was there, on a Sunday, after he had celebrated Mass, the venerable saint said to his sister, and to the brothers who were with him, 'My very dear friends, today the Lord my God summons me to eternal life, and I order you, in the name of Christ, to do exactly what I tell you now, if you want my blessing.

'Conceal my death here, until my body has been carried to my own city of Clonfert, because there will be the place of my resurrection. If the people here come to know of my death amongst them, they will surely bury me here, against my wishes. You must, therefore, place my corpse in a wagon, and carefully cover it over.

'Only one brother should be in charge of the wagon, and he will tell anyone who asks him that he is carrying the goods of St Brendan to his own city of Clonfert. In that way, everyone will let him pass, except one man, a soldier, named Curryn, who is blind in his left eye.

'This man will not believe the words of the brother, but will question him cunningly about what he is carrying so secretly, and will carefully search the wagon. When he finds my body, he will order the brother to leave it right there. He will say to me, "You will be buried with all honour here in our country, so that your resurrection may be among us, man of God."

'Then the brother with the wagon will look into a trench beside him, and see a lump of pure gold. He will offer it to this soldier, saying, "Take this gold given by God, and let me pass on."

'This the man will refuse, and then the brother will promise, "You will have the chief power in your tribe, and your children after you, if you allow me to pass."

But the man will still prevent his passing; and then the brother will say to him, "You will not have eternal life, unless you permit the saint of God to be carried to the place where he wanted to be buried. You must believe me, because I know that when you met me, you were secretly planning to become the chief of your tribe by murdering members of your own family."

'When the man hears the secret thoughts of his heart told to him by a stranger, he will allow the brother to proceed in peace with my body, who will bless him, and go on his way rejoicing.'

When Brendan's sister and the monks heard this prediction of what was going to happen, they promised the holy father that they would do what he had commanded.

Soon after this, Brendan gave his blessing to his sister and the monks, and, going on to the convent, went inside. There he raised his eyes to heaven and said, 'Into Thy hands, Lord, I commend my soul; save me, Lord, my God,' and then the aged most holy Brendan gave his soul to God, on Sunday, May the sixteenth; having completed the ninety-third year of his age.

His corpse was placed on a wagon, and one brother was put in charge of it, as the saint had directed, and everything occurred as he had foretold. A great number of holy men assembled from all quarters on the occasion, and his blessed body was buried in the place of honour, with all glory and reverence; with psalmody and spiritual canticles; our Lord Jesus Christ reigning over heaven and earth, and all creatures, in union with the Father and Holy Spirit, for ever and ever. Amen.

Further Reading

Homer, *The Odyssey* (translated by E.V. Rieu), Penguin, 2003

Irving, Washington, *A History of the Life and Voyages of Christopher Columbus*, John Murray, 1828

O'Donoghue, Denis: *Brendaniana: St. Brendan the Voyager in Story and Legend*, Browne & Nolan, 1893

Rolleston, T.W.: *Myths & Legends of the Celtic Race*, Harrap, 1911

Severin, Tim: *The Brendan Voyage*, Gill & Macmillan, 2005

Webb, J.F., *The Age of Bede*, Penguin, 1998

Yeats, W.B.: *Fairy and Folk Tales of the Irish Peasantry*, Walter Scott, 1888

For free downloads, and for more books from the Langley Press, please visit our website at:

http://tinyurl.com/lpdirect

Made in the USA
Middletown, DE
03 November 2023

41931930R00047